FUN FASHIONS for girls

Her fashion dolls shouldn't have all the dress-up fun—not when you can quickly crochet 14 easy designs for the young stylista's wardrobe! Sweet details like crocheted flowers and bold buttons highlight a number of gotta-have-'em garments and accessories. Instructions for the cool tops are written in sizes 2 through 6. Matching hats and handbags join a pair of hand mitts and a ruffle-trimmed shrug to round out the collection. Now your little miss will have plenty of fun fashions to model every day!

LEISURE ARTS, INC.
Little Rock, Arkansas

HOT PINK SET

Shown on pages 3, 5, and 6.

EASY

Finished Size

BAG: 7 1/2" (19 cm) tall
HAT: 18 1/2" (47 cm) circumference
HAND MITTS: 6" (15 cm) long, 7 1/2{8 3/4}"/19{22} cm circumference

Size Note: Hand Mitts are written for size 2/4 with size 6 in braces { }. Instructions will be easier to read if you circle all the numbers pertaining to your child's size. If only one number is given, it applies to both sizes.

MATERIALS

SET

100% Cotton Medium Weight Yarn (MEDIUM 4)
[2 1/2 ounces, 120 yards
(71 grams, 109 meters) per ball]:
Pink - 2 balls
White **and** Black - 1 ball **each**

BAG

Crochet hook, size G (4 mm) **or** size needed for gauge
25" (63.5 cm) length Black ribbon
1/2" (12 mm) Black buttons - 9
Yarn needle
Sewing needle and black thread

HAT

Crochet hook, size H (5 mm) **or** size needed for gauge
1/2" (12 mm) Black buttons - 6
1/2" (12 mm) White buttons - 6
Sewing needle and black & white thread

HAND MITTS

Crochet hook, size G (4 mm) **or** size needed for gauge

Instructions begin on page 4.

GAUGES

Bag: In pattern,
Worked through Rnd 4 = $4\frac{3}{4}$" (12 cm)

Hat: In pattern,
Worked through Rnd 3 = $3\frac{1}{4}$" (8.25 cm)

Hand Mitts: In pattern, 8 sts = $2\frac{1}{2}$" (6.25 cm);
6 rnds = $2\frac{3}{4}$" (7 cm)

Gauge Swatches

Bag: $4\frac{3}{4}$" (12 cm) diameter
Work same as Bag through Rnd 4.

Hat: $3\frac{1}{4}$" (8.25 cm) diameter
Work same as Hat through Rnd 3.

Hand Mitts: $2\frac{1}{2}$" x $2\frac{3}{4}$"
(6.25 cm x 7 cm)

Ch 10.

Row 1: Dc in fourth ch from hook and in each ch across **(3 skipped chs count as first dc)**: 8 dc.

Rows 2-6: Ch 3 **(counts as first dc)**, turn; dc in next dc and in each dc across. Finish off.

STITCH GUIDE

FRONT POST DOUBLE CROCHET

(abbreviated FPdc)

YO, insert hook from **front** to **back** around post of st indicated *(Fig. A)*, YO and pull up a loop, (YO and draw through 2 loops on hook) twice.

Fig. A

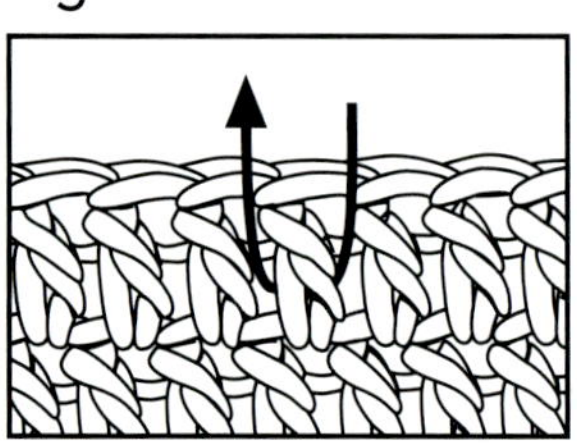

BAG

With Black, ch 4; join with slip st to form a ring.

Rnd 1 (Right side)**:** Ch 3 **(counts as first dc, now and throughout)**, 15 dc in ring; join with slip st to first dc: 16 dc.

Note: Loop a short piece of yarn around any stitch to mark Rnd 1 as **right** side.

Rnd 2: Ch 3, dc in same st, 2 dc in next dc and in each dc around; join with slip st to first dc: 32 dc.

Rnd 3: Ch 3, dc in same st and in next dc, (2 dc in next dc, dc in next dc) around; join with slip st to first dc: 48 dc.

Rnd 4: Ch 3, dc in same st and in next 2 dc, (2 dc in next dc, dc in next 2 dc) around; join with slip st to first dc, finish off: 64 dc.

Rnd 5: With **right** side facing, join Pink with dc in same st as joining ***(see Joining With Dc, page 32)***; dc in Back Loop Only of next dc and each dc around ***(Fig. 1, page 32)***; join with slip st to first dc.

Rnds 6 and 7: Ch 3, dc in both loops of next dc and each dc around; join with slip st to first dc.

Finish off.

Rnd 8: With **right** side facing, join White with sc in same st as joining ***(see Joining With Sc, page 32)***; sc in next dc and in each dc around; join with slip st to first sc.

Rnd 9: Ch 1, sc in same st and in each sc around; join with slip st to first sc, finish off.

Rnd 10: With **right** side facing, join Pink with dc in same st as joining; dc in next sc and in each sc around; join with slip st to first dc.

Instructions continued on page 6.

Instructions can be found on the following pages from left to right—Hot Pink Hat, page 6; Ruffled Hat, page 30; Rose Motif Hat, page 27; Watermelon Hat, page 23.

Rnds 11 and 12: Ch 3, dc in next dc and in each dc around; join with slip st to first dc.

Finish off.

Rnds 13-21: Repeat Rnds 8-12 once, then repeat Rnds 8-11 once **more**.

Rnd 22: Ch 3, dc in same st and in next 31 dc, 2 dc in next dc, dc in next dc and in each dc around; join with slip st to first dc, finish off: 66 dc.

Rnd 23: With **right** side facing, join Black with sc in same st as joining; skip next 2 dc, 7 dc in next dc, skip next 2 dc, ★ sc in next dc, skip next 2 dc, 7 dc in next dc, skip next 2 dc; repeat from ★ around; join with slip st to first sc, finish off.

HANDLE

With Black, ch 91.

Row 1: Sc in second ch from hook and in each ch across; finish off.

FINISHING

With **right** side of Bag facing, skip first three 7-dc groups on Rnd 23 and sew one end of Handle to center dc of next 7-dc group; skip next four 7-dc groups and sew other end of Handle to center dc of next 7-dc group.

Sew buttons randomly to right side of Bag.

Weave ribbon through dc on Rnd 21 working under and over 2 dc at a time; gather and tie into a bow.

HAT

With Pink, ch 4; join with slip st to form a ring.

Rnd 1 (Right side)**:** Ch 3 **(counts as first dc, now and throughout)**, 11 dc in ring; join with slip st to first dc: 12 dc.

Note: Loop a short piece of yarn around any stitch to mark Rnd 1 as **right** side.

Rnd 2: Ch 3, dc in same st, 2 dc in next dc and in each dc around; join with slip st to first dc: 24 dc.

Rnd 3: Ch 3, dc in next dc, work FPdc around **same** dc worked into, (dc in next 2 dc, work FPdc around **same** dc worked into) around; join with slip st to first dc: 36 sts.

Rnd 4: Ch 3, dc in next 2 sts, work FPdc around **same** st worked into, (dc in next 3 sts, work FPdc around **same** st worked into) around; join with slip st to first dc: 48 sts.

Rnd 5: Ch 3, dc in next 3 sts, work FPdc around **same** st worked into, (dc in next 4 sts, work FPdc around **same** st worked into) around; join with slip st to first dc: 60 dc.

Rnds 6-14: Ch 3, dc in next 3 dc, work FPdc around next FPdc, (dc in next 4 dc, work FPdc around next FPdc) around; join with slip st to first dc.

Finish off.

Rnd 15: With **right** side facing, join White with sc in same st as joining; sc in next dc and in each st around; join with slip st to first sc, finish off.

Rnd 16: With **right** side facing, join Black with sc in same st as joining; sc in next sc and in each sc around; join with slip st to first sc, finish off.

With **right** side facing and alternating colors, sew buttons between FPdc on Rnd 13.

HAND MITT (Make 2)

With Pink, ch 24{28}; being careful not to twist ch, join with slip st to form a ring.

Rnd 1 (Right side)**:** Ch 1, sc same ch and in each ch around; join with slip st to first sc: 24{28} sc.

Note: Loop a short piece of yarn around any stitch to mark Rnd 1 as **right** side.

Rnd 2: Ch 1, sc in same st and in each sc around; join with slip st to first sc.

Rnd 3: Ch 3 **(counts as first dc, now and throughout)**, dc in next sc and in each sc around; join with slip st to first dc.

Rnd 4: Ch 3, dc in next 2 dc, work FPdc around next dc, (dc in next 3 dc, work FPdc around next dc) around; join with slip st to first dc.

Rnds 5-11: Ch 3, dc in next 2 dc, work FPdc around next FPdc, (dc in next 3 dc, work FPdc around next FPdc) around; join with slip st to first dc.

Rnd 12: Ch 1, sc in same st and in each st around; join with slip st to first sc.

Rnd 13: Ch 1, sc in same st and in next 6 sc, ch 3, skip next 3 sc, sc in next sc and in each sc around; join with slip st to first sc: 21{25} sc and one ch-3 sp.

Rnd 14: Ch 1, sc in same st and in next 6 sc, 3 sc in next ch-3 sp, sc in next sc and in each sc around; join with slip st to first sc, finish off: 24{28} sc.

Rnd 15: With **right** side facing, join White with sc in same st as joining; sc in next sc and in each sc around; join with slip st to first sc, finish off.

Rnd 16: With **right** side facing, join Black with sc in same st as joining; sc in next sc and in each sc around; join with slip st to first sc, finish off.

BOTTOM TRIM

Rnd 1: With **right** side facing and working in free loops of beginning ch ***(Fig. 3, page 32)***, join White with sc in any ch; sc in next ch and in each ch around; join with slip st to first sc, finish off: 24{28} sc.

Rnd 2: With **right** side facing, join Black with sc in same st as joining; sc in next sc and in each sc around; join with slip st to first sc, finish off.

BROWN FLOWER SET

EASY

Finished Size

Purse: $6\frac{1}{2}$" x $8\frac{1}{2}$" (16.5 cm x 21.5 cm), excluding handle
Hat: 21" (53.5 cm) circumference

MATERIALS

100% Cotton Medium Weight Yarn (MEDIUM 4)
[$2\frac{1}{2}$ ounces, 120 yards
(70 grams, 109 meters) per ball]:
Brown - 2 balls
Orange, Pink, **and** Blue - 1 ball **each**
Green - small amount (for Tassel)
Crochet hook, sizes H (5 mm) **and** I (5.5 mm) **or**
sizes needed for gauge
$\frac{1}{2}$" (12 mm) Assorted color buttons - 10
Yarn needle
Sewing needle and thread

GAUGE: With smaller size hook, 8 sc and 8 rows = 2" (5 cm)

Gauge Swatch: 2" (5 cm) square
With smaller size hook, ch 9.
Row 1: Sc in second ch from hook and in each ch across: 8 sc.
Rows 2-8: Ch 1, turn; sc in each sc across.
Finish off.

STITCH GUIDE

Treble Crochet *(abbreviated tr)*
YO twice, insert hook in st indicated, YO and pull up a loop, (4 loops on hook), (YO and draw through 2 loops on hook) 3 times.

Instructions begin on page 10.

PURSE

FRONT

With smaller size hook and Brown, ch 25.

Row 1 (Right side)**:** Sc in second ch from hook and in each ch across: 24 sc.

Note: Loop a short piece of yarn around any stitch to mark Row 1 as **right** side.

Rows 2-34: Ch 1, turn; sc in each sc across.

Finish off.

BACK

Work same as Front.

FLAP

Row 1: With **right** side of Back facing, smaller size hook, and working in Back Loops Only *(Fig. 1, page 32)*, skip first 3 sc and join Brown with sc in next sc *(see Joining With Sc, page 32)*; sc in next 17 sc, leave remaining 3 sc unworked: 18 sc.

Rows 2-14: Ch 1, turn; sc in each sc across.

Finish off.

With **right** side facing and working in end of rows on Flap, join Brown with sc in first row; ch 1, work 14 sc evenly spaced across; working across Row 14, 3 sc in first sc, sc in each sc across to last sc, 3 sc in last sc; work 14 sc evenly spaced across end of rows; finish off.

HANDLE

With smaller size hook and Brown, ch 90.

Row 1: Sc in second ch from hook and in each ch across; finish off.

TASSEL

Cut a piece of cardboard 3" (7.5 cm) wide and 9" (23 cm) long. Holding one strand each of Brown, Pink, Orange, and Green, wind yarn around the cardboard approximately 12 times.

Cut a 20" (51 cm) length of Brown and insert it under all of the strands at the top of the cardboard; pull up **tightly** and tie securely. Make a slip knot on one long end near top of tassel. With Brown, ch 10; slip st at base of first ch, finish off.

Cut the yarn at the opposite end of the cardboard and then remove it *(Fig. A)*. Cut a 6" (15 cm) length of Brown and wrap it **tightly** around the tassel twice, $1^{1}/_{2}$" (4 cm) below the top *(Fig. B)*; tie securely. Trim the ends.

Fig. A

Fig. B

FLOWER

With Orange and smaller size hook, ch 4; join with slip st to form a ring.

Rnd 1 (Right side)**:** (Ch 3, 2 tr, ch 3, slip st) 6 times in ring; finish off.

With Pink, repeat for second Flower.

FINISHING

Sew Pink Flower to bottom right corner of Front. Sew button to center of Flower.

With **wrong** sides of Front and Back together, Front facing, smaller size hook, and working in end of rows through **both** thicknesses, join Brown with sc in end of Row 34; work 29 sc evenly spaced across; working in free loops of beginning ch *(Fig. 3, page 32)*, 3 sc in first ch, sc in next 22 chs, 3 sc in next ch; work 30 sc evenly spaced across end of rows; finish off.

With Brown, sew one end of Handle to joining. Place Tassel on Handle. Being careful not to twist Handle, sew second end to joining at other side of Purse.

With **right** side facing and using photo as a guide, sew Orange Flower to Flap. With sewing needle and thread, sew one button to center of Flower. Sew remaining buttons randomly to Flap.

HAT

With larger size hook and Brown, ch 5; join with slip st to form a ring.

Rnd 1 (Right side)**:** Ch 3 **(counts as first dc, now and throughout)**, 17 dc in ring; join with slip st to first dc: 18 dc.

Note: Loop a short piece of yarn around any stitch to mark Rnd 1 as **right** side.

Rnd 2: Ch 4 **(counts as first dc plus ch 1, now and throughout)**, (dc in next dc, ch 1) around; join with slip st to first dc, finish off: 18 dc and 18 ch-1 sps.

Rnd 3: With **right** side facing, join Orange with dc in any ch-1 sp *(see Joining With Dc, page 32)*; ch 1, (3 dc in next ch-1 sp, ch 1) around, 2 dc in same sp as first dc; join with slip st to first dc: 54 dc and 18 ch-1 sps.

Rnd 4: (Slip st, ch 3, 2 dc) in first ch-1 sp, ch 1, (3 dc in next ch-1 sp, ch 1) around; join with slip st to first dc, finish off.

Rnd 5: With **right** side facing, join Brown with dc in any ch-1 sp; 2 dc in same sp, ch 1, (3 dc in next ch-1 sp, ch 1) around; join with slip st to first dc, finish off.

Rnd 6: With **right** side facing, join Pink with dc in any ch-1 sp; ch 1, (3 dc in next ch-1 sp, ch 1) around, 2 dc in same sp as first dc; join with slip st to first dc.

Rnd 7: (Slip st, ch 3, 2 dc) in first ch-1 sp, ch 1, (3 dc in next ch-1 sp, ch 1) around; join with slip st to first dc, finish off.

Rnd 8: With **right** side facing, join Brown with dc in any ch-1 sp; 2 dc in same sp, ch 1, (3 dc in next ch-1 sp, ch 1) around; join with slip st to first dc, finish off.

Rnd 9: With **right** side facing, join Blue with dc in any ch-1 sp; ch 1, (3 dc in next ch-1 sp, ch 1) around, 2 dc in same sp as first dc; join with slip st to first dc.

Rnd 10: (Slip st, ch 3, 2 dc) in first ch-1 sp, ch 1, (3 dc in next ch-1 sp, ch 1) around; join with slip st to first dc, finish off.

Rnd 11: With **right** side facing, join Brown with sc in any dc *(see Joining With Sc, page 32)*; sc in each dc and in each ch-1 sp around; join with slip st to first sc: 72 sc.

Rnds 12-14: Ch 1, sc in same st and in each sc around; join with slip st to first sc.

Finish off.

CAMOUFLAGE APRON

EASY

Size	To Fit Chest Measurement
2	20-22" (51-56 cm)
4	22-24" (56-61 cm)
6	24-26" (61-66 cm)

Size Note: Instructions are written for size 2 with sizes 4 and 6 in braces { }. Instructions will be easier to read if you circle all the numbers pertaining to your child's size. If only one number is given, it applies to all sizes.

MATERIALS

MEDIUM 4

Medium Weight Yarn
  [3½ ounces, 195 yards
  (100 grams, 175 meters) per skein]:
    Variegated - 1{2-2} skein(s)
100% Cotton Medium Weight Yarn
  [2½ ounces, 120 yards
  (70 grams, 109 meters) per ball]:
    Ecru - small amount
Crochet hook, size H (5 mm) **or** size needed for gauge
½" (12 mm) Wooden button
Yarn needle
Tapestry needle

Instructions begin on page 14.

GAUGE: 8 dc and 4 rows = 2" (5 cm)

Gauge Swatch: 2" (5 cm) square
Ch 10.
Row 1: Dc in fourth ch from hook and in each ch across **(3 skipped chs count as first dc)**: 8 dc.
Rows 2-4: Ch 3 **(counts as first dc)**, turn; dc in next dc and in each dc across.
Finish off.

STITCH GUIDE

Treble Crochet *(abbreviated tr)*
YO twice, insert hook in st indicated, YO and pull up a loop, (4 loops on hook), (YO and draw through 2 loops on hook) 3 times.

APRON

BODICE

With Variegated, ch 29{31-33}.

Row 1: Dc in fourth ch from hook and in each ch across **(3 skipped chs count as first dc)**: 27{29-31} dc.

Row 2 (Right side)**:** Ch 3 **(count as first dc, now and throughout)**, turn; dc in same st and in each dc across to last dc, 2 dc in last dc: 29{31-33} dc.

Note: Loop a short piece of yarn around any stitch to mark Row 2 as **right** side.

Rows 3 thru 9{10-11}: Ch 3, turn; dc in same st and in each dc across to last dc, 2 dc in last dc: 43{47-51} dc.

Finish off.

SKIRT

With Variegated, ch 70{78-86}.

Row 1: Sc in second ch from hook and in each ch across: 69{77-85} sc.

Row 2 (Right side)**:** Ch 4 **(counts as first tr, now and throughout)**, turn; 3 tr in same st, skip next 3 sc, sc in next sc, ★ skip next 3 sc, 7 tr in next sc, skip next 3 sc, sc in next sc; repeat from ★ across.

Note: Mark Row 2 as **right** side.

Rows 3 thru 12{12-14}: Ch 4, turn; 3 tr in same st, skip next 3 tr, sc in next tr, ★ 7 tr in next sc, skip next 3 tr, sc in next tr; repeat from ★ across.

Row 13{13-15}: Ch 1, turn; sc in each st across; finish off.

FLOWER

With Variegated, ch 4; join with slip st to form a ring.

Rnd 1 (Right side)**:** Ch 3, 13 dc in ring; join with slip st to first dc, finish off: 14 dc.

Note: Mark Rnd 1 as **right** side.

Rnd 2: With **right** side facing, join Ecru with slip st in any dc; ch 5, skip next dc, ★ slip st in next dc, ch 5, skip next dc; repeat from ★ around, join with slip st to joining slip st: 7 ch-5 sps.

Rnd 3: ★ (Slip st, ch 3, 6 dc) in next ch-5 sp, slip st in next dc on Rnd 1 working around slip st on Rnd 2; repeat from ★ around; join with slip st to first slip st, finish off.

JOINING

Working through **both** loops of dc on last row of Bodice **and** through free loops of beginning ch on Skirt *(Fig. 3, page 32)*, center Bodice on Skirt, leaving 13{15-17} sts unworked on each side and whipstitch pieces together *(Fig. 4, page 32)*.

With **right** side facing, join Variegated with sc in end of last row on Skirt *(see Joining With Sc, page 32)*; work 29{29-32} sc evenly spaced across end of rows, ch 45, slip st in second ch from hook and in each ch across (waist tie); working in free loops of beginning ch on Skirt, sc in each ch across to joining; working in end of rows on Bodice, work 17{18-19} sc evenly spaced across, ch 50, slip st in second ch from hook and in each ch across (neck tie); working in free loops of beginning ch on Bodice, work 25{27-29} sc evenly spaced across, ch 50, slip st in second ch from hook and in each ch across (neck tie); working in end of rows on Bodice, work 17{18-19} sc evenly spaced across; working in free loops of beginning ch on Skirt, sc in each ch across, ch 45, slip st in second ch from hook and in each ch across (waist tie); working in end of rows on Skirt, work 30{30-33} sc evenly spaced across; slip st in end of last row on Skirt; finish off.

Using photo as a guide and one strand of Ecru, sew button to center of Flower. With Variegated, sew Flower to Bodice.

PRETTY POSIES SET

EASY

Size	Finished Chest Measurement
2	19" (48.5 cm)
4	20" (51 cm)
6	21" (53.5 cm)

Kerchief: 13" (33 cm) across front edge;
10¾" (27.5 cm) from front edge to point

Size Note: Instructions are written for size 2 with sizes 4 and 6 in braces { }. Instructions will be easier to read if you circle all the numbers pertaining to your child's size. If only one number is given, it applies to all sizes.

MATERIALS

- Medium Weight Yarn
  - [3½ ounces, 178 yards (100 grams, 163 meters) per skein]:
    - Lavender - 3 skeins
    - Pink, Green, **and** White - 1 skein **each**
- Crochet hook, sizes H (5 mm) **and** I (5.5 mm) **or** sizes needed for gauge
- Pony beads:
  - Pink - 5
  - Green **and** Purple - 4 **each**
- Split-ring markers - 4
- Yarn needle

Instructions begin on page 18.

GAUGE: With smaller size hook,
in Bodice pattern,
8 sts and 7 rows = 2" (5 cm)

Gauge Swatch: 2" (5 cm) square
With smaller size hook, ch 9.
Row 1: Sc in second ch from hook and in each ch across: 8 sc.
Row 2: Ch 1, turn; sc in each sc across.
Row 3: Ch 2 **(counts as first hdc, now and throughout)**, turn; hdc in next sc and in each sc across.
Rows 4-6: Ch 1, turn; sc in each st across.
Row 7: Ch 2, turn; hdc in next sc and in each sc across.
Finish off.

STITCH GUIDE

V-STITCH *(abbreviated V-St)*
(Dc, ch 1, dc) in st or sp indicated.
DECREASE
(uses next 2 sts)
★ YO, insert hook in **next** st, YO and pull up a loop, YO and draw through 2 loops on hook; repeat from ★ once **more**, YO and draw through all 3 loops on hook **(counts as one dc)**.

TOP

BODICE

With smaller size hook and Purple, ch 76{80-84} **loosely**; being careful **not** to twist ch, join with slip st to form a ring.

Rnd 1 (Right side)**:** Ch 1, sc in same ch and in each ch around; join with slip st to first sc: 76{80-84} sc.

Note: Loop a short piece of yarn around any stitch to mark Rnd 1 as **right** side.

Rnd 2: Ch 1, sc in same st and in each sc around; join with slip st to first sc, finish off.

Rnd 3: With **right** side facing, join Pink with slip st in same st as joining; ch 2 **(counts as first hdc, now and throughout)**, hdc in next sc and in each sc around; join with slip st to first hdc, finish off.

Rnd 4: With **right** side facing, join Green with sc in same st as joining *(see Joining With Sc, page 32)*; sc in next hdc and in each hdc around; join with slip st to first sc.

Rnds 5 and 6: Ch 1, sc in same st and in each sc around; join with slip st to first sc.

Finish off.

Rnd 7: With **right** side facing, join White with slip st in same st as joining; ch 2, hdc in next sc and in each sc around; join with slip st to first hdc, finish off.

Rnd 8: With **right** side facing, join Purple with sc in same st as joining; sc in next hdc and in each hdc around; join with slip st to first sc.

Rnd 9: Ch 1, sc in same st and in each sc around; join with slip st to first sc, finish off.

Rnd 10: With **right** side facing, join Pink with slip st in same st as joining; ch 2, hdc in next sc and in each sc around; join with slip st to first hdc.

Rnd 11: Ch 2, hdc in next hdc and in each hdc around; join with slip st to first hdc, finish off.

Rnd 12: With **right** side facing, join Green with sc in same st as joining; sc in next hdc and in each hdc around; join with slip st to first sc.

Rnd 13: Ch 1, sc in same st and in each sc around; join with slip st to first sc, finish off.

Rnd 14: With **right** side facing, join White with sc in same st as joining; sc in next sc and in each sc around; join with slip st to first sc.

Rnds 15 and 16: Ch 1, sc in same st and in each sc around; join with slip st to first sc.

Finish off.

SKIRT

Rnd 1: With **right** side facing and larger size hook, join Purple with slip st in same st as joining; ch 3 **(counts as first dc)**, dc in same st and in next sc, (2 dc in next sc, dc in next sc) around; join with slip st to first dc: 114{120-126} dc.

Rnd 2: Ch 4 **(counts as first dc plus ch 1, now and throughout)**, dc in same st, skip next dc, (work V-St in next dc, skip next dc) around; join with slip st to first dc: 57{60-63} V-Sts.

Rnds 3-12: Slip st in next ch-1 sp, ch 4, dc in same sp, work V-St in next ch-1 sp and in each ch-1 sp around; join with slip st to first dc.

Rnd 13: Ch 1, sc in same st and in each ch-1 sp and each dc around; join with slip st to first sc, finish off: 171{180-189} sc.

Rnd 14: With **right** side facing, join Pink with sc in same st as joining; sc in each sc around; join with slip st to first sc.

Rnd 15: Ch 1, sc in same st and in each sc around; join with slip st to first sc, finish off.

Rnd 16: With **right** side facing, join Green with slip st in same st as joining; ch 1, working from **left** to **right**, work reverse sc in each st around ***(Figs. 5a-d, page 33)***; join with slip st to first st, finish off.

Trim: With **right** side facing, using smaller size hook, working around beginning ch and in sps **between** sc on Rnd 1 of Bodice ***(Fig. 2, page 32)***, join White with slip st in any sp; ch 1, working from **left** to **right**, work reverse sc in each sp around; join with slip st to first st, finish off.

SHOULDER TIES

With Trim at top and joinings at back, flatten Bodice. Place markers 1¾{2½-3}"/4.5{6.5-7.5} cm from folded edge on **each** side of front and back.

String one each Green, Purple, and Pink pony bead onto White yarn. With **right** side facing, using smaller size hook, working **around** Trim and into sps **between** sc on Rnd 1 of Bodice, join White with slip st at any marker; ch 42{47-47}, mark last ch made for st placement, slide up bead, ch 1, slide up bead, ch 1, slide up bead, ch 1, slip st in marked ch, sc in next ch and in each ch across, slip st in same st as joining slip st; finish off.

Repeat for remaining 3 Shoulder Ties.

FLOWER

With smaller size hook and White, ch 4; join with slip st to form a ring.

Rnd 1 (Right side)**:** Ch 3, 17 dc in ring; join with slip st to first dc, finish off: 18 dc.

Note: Mark Rnd 1 as **right** side.

Rnd 2: With **right** side facing, join Green with slip st in same st as joining; ch 5, skip next 2 dc, ★ slip st in next dc, ch 5, skip next 2 dc; repeat from ★ around; join with slip st to first slip st: 6 ch-5 sps.

Rnd 3: ★ 6 Sc in next ch-5 sp, slip st in next dc on Rnd 1 working around slip st on Rnd 2; repeat from ★ around; join with slip st to first sc, finish off.

Rnd 4: With **right** side facing and working **behind** Rnds 2 and 3 and in skipped dc on Rnd 1, join Purple with slip st in first skipped dc on Rnd 1; ch 8, skip next skipped dc, (slip st in next skipped dc, ch 8, skip next skipped dc) around; join with slip st to joining slip st: 6 ch-8 sps.

Rnd 5: ★ 9 Sc in next ch-8 sp, slip st in next dc on Rnd 1 working around slip st on Rnd 4; repeat from ★ around; join with slip st to first slip st, finish off.

With White, sew Pink pony bead to center of Flower; sew Flower to front of Bodice.

KERCHIEF

BODY

With smaller size hook and Lavender, ch 51.

Row 1 (Right side)**:** Sc in second ch from hook and in each ch across: 50 sc.

Note: Mark Row 1 as **right** side.

Row 2: Ch 3 **(counts as first dc, now and throughout)**, turn; decrease, dc in next sc and in each sc across to last 3 sc, decrease, dc in last sc: 48 dc.

Row 3: Ch 4 **(counts as first dc plus ch 1)**, turn; ★ skip next dc, dc in next dc, ch 1; repeat from ★ across to last 3 dc, skip next 2 dc, dc in last dc: 24 dc and 23 chs.

Row 4: Ch 3, turn; decrease, dc in next ch and in each dc and each ch across to last 2 chs, decrease, skip last ch, dc in last dc: 44 dc.

Rows 5-22: Repeat Rows 3 and 4, 9 times: 8 dc.

Trim: Ch 1, turn; sc in each dc across; work 49 sc evenly spaced across end of rows; ch 40, slip st in second ch from hook and in each ch across; working around beginning ch and in sps **between** sc on Rnd 1, sc in each sp across; ch 40, slip st in second ch from hook and in each ch across; work 49 sc evenly spaced across end of rows; join with slip st to first sc, finish off.

WATERMELON SET

EASY

Size	Finished Chest Measurement
2	$19^{1}/_{2}$" (49.5 cm)
4	22" (56 cm)
6	24" (61 cm)

Hat: 18" (45.5 cm) circumference

Size Note: Instructions are written for size 2 with sizes 4 and 6 in braces { }. Instructions will be easier to read if you circle all the numbers pertaining to your child's size. If only one number is given, it applies to all sizes.

MATERIALS

MEDIUM 4

Medium Weight Yarn
[$3^{1}/_{2}$ ounces, 178 yards
(100 grams, 163 meters) per skein]:
Pink - 2 skeins
Green **and** White - 1 skein **each**
Crochet hook, sizes G (4 mm) **and** I (5.5 mm)
or sizes needed for gauge
Pony beads - 6 Black
Markers - 4
Yarn needle

Instructions begin on page 22.

GAUGE

Top: With larger size hook,
in Bodice pattern,
11 sts and 10 rows = 3" (7.5 cm)
Hat: Rnds 1-3 = 4½" (11.5 cm)

Gauge Swatch: 3" (7.5 cm) square
With larger size hook, ch 12.
Row 1: Sc in second ch from hook and in each ch across: 11 sc.
Row 2: Ch 2 **(counts as first hdc)**, turn; hdc in next sc and in each sc across.
Row 3: Ch 1, turn; sc in each hdc across.
Rows 4-10: Repeat Rows 2 and 3, 3 times; then repeat Row 2 once **more**.
Finish off.

STITCH GUIDE

V-STITCH *(abbreviated V-St)*
(Dc, ch 1, dc) in st or sp indicated.

TOP

BODICE

With larger size hook and Green, ch 72{80-88} **loosely**; being careful **not** to twist ch, join with slip st to form a ring.

Rnd 1 (Right side)**:** Ch 1, sc in same ch and in each ch around; join with slip st to first sc: 72{80-88} sc.

Note: Loop a short piece of yarn around any stitch to mark Rnd 1 as **right** side.

Rnd 2: Ch 2 **(counts as first hdc)**, hdc in next sc and in each sc around; join with slip st to first hdc.

Rnd 3: Ch 1, sc in same st and in each hdc around; join with slip st to first sc.

Rnds 4 thru 11{13-15}: Repeat Rnds 2 and 3, 4{5-6} times.

Finish off.

SKIRT

Rnd 1: With **right** side facing, join Pink with slip st in same st as joining; ch 4 **(counts as first dc plus ch 1, now and throughout)**, dc in same st, skip next sc, (work V-St in next sc, skip next sc) around; join with slip st to first dc: 36{40-44} V-Sts.

Rnds 2-10: Slip st in first ch-1 sp, ch 4, dc in same sp, work V-St in next ch-1 sp and in each ch-1 sp around; join with slip st to first dc.

Rnd 11: Ch 1, sc in same st and in each ch-1 sp and each dc around; join with slip st to first sc, finish off: 108{120-132} sc.

Rnd 12: With **right** side facing, join White with sc in same st as joining *(see Joining With Sc, page 32)*; sc in each sc around; join with slip st to first sc.

Rnd 13: Ch 1, sc in same st and in each sc around; join with slip st to first sc, finish off.

Rnd 14: With **right** side facing, join Green with sc in same st as joining; sc in next 4 sc, (slip st, ch 4, slip st) in next sc, ★ sc in next 5 sc, (slip st, ch 4, slip st) in next sc; repeat from ★ around; join with slip st to first sc, finish off.

TRIM

With **right** side facing, using larger size hook, working around beginning ch and in sps **between** sc on Rnd 1 of Bodice *(Fig. 2, page 32)*, join White with slip st in any sp; ch 1, work reverse sc in each sp around *(Figs. 5a-d, page 33)*; join with slip st to first st, finish off.

SHOULDER TIES

With Trim at top and joinings at back, flatten Bodice. Place markers 2¼{2¾-3¼}"/5.5{7-8.5} cm from folded edge on **each** side of front and back.

With **right** side facing, using larger size hook, working **around** Trim and in sps **between** sc on Rnd 1 of Bodice, join Pink with slip st at any marker; ch 42{44-46}, sc in second ch from hook and in each ch across, slip st in same st as joining slip st; finish off.

Repeat for remaining 3 Shoulder Ties.

WATERMELON SLICE

FLESH

With smaller size hook and Pink, ch 2.

Row 1 (Right side)**:** Sc in second ch from hook.

Note: Mark Row 1 as **right** side.

Row 2: Ch 1, turn; 2 sc in sc: 2 sc.

Row 3: Ch 1, turn; sc in first sc, 2 sc in last sc: 3 sc.

Rows 4-11: Ch 1, turn; sc in each sc across to last sc, 2 sc in last sc: 11 sc.

Trim: Ch 1, do **not** turn; work 11 sc evenly spaced across end of rows, 3 sc in free loop of beginning ch *(Fig. 3, page 32)*, work 11 sc evenly spaced across end of rows, slip st in first sc on Row 11; finish off.

RIND

Row 1: With **right** side facing, join White with sc in end of Trim; sc in each sc across Row 11, sc in end of Trim; finish off: 13 sc.

Row 2: With **right** side facing, join Green with sc in first sc; sc in each sc across; finish off.

Using photo as a guide:
With yarn needle and Pink, sew Black pony beads to **right** side of Watermelon Slice.
With Pink, sew Watermelon Slice to front of Bodice.

HAT

Shown on page 6.

With larger size hook and Pink, ch 5; join with slip st to form a ring.

Rnd 1 (Right side)**:** Ch 3 **(counts as first dc, now and throughout)**, 17 dc in ring; join with slip st to first dc: 18 dc.

Note: Loop a short piece of yarn around any stitch to mark Rnd 1 as **right** side.

Rnd 2: Ch 4 **(counts as first dc plus ch 1, now and throughout)**, (dc in next dc, ch 1) around; join with slip st to first dc: 18 dc and 18 ch-1 sps.

Rnds 3-10: Slip st in first ch-1 sp, ch 4, (3 dc in next ch-1 sp, ch 1) around, 2 dc in same sp as first dc; join with slip st to first dc: 54 dc and 18 ch-1 sps.

Rnd 11: Slip st in first ch-1 sp, ch 3, 2 dc in same sp, ch 1, (3 dc in next ch-1 sp, ch 1) around; join with slip st to first dc.

Rnd 12: Ch 1, sc in same st and in each dc and each ch-1 sp around; join with slip st to first sc, finish off: 72 sc.

Rnd 13: With **right** side facing, join White with sc same st as joining *(see Joining With Sc, page 32)*; sc in next sc and in each sc around; join with slip st to first sc, finish off.

Rnd 14: With **right** side facing, join Green with sc in same st as joining; sc in next sc and in each sc around; join with slip st to first sc.

Rnd 15: Ch 1, sc in same st and in next 4 sc, (slip st, ch 4, slip st) in next sc, ★ sc in next 5 sc, (slip st, ch 4, slip st) in next sc; repeat from ★ around; join with slip st to first sc, finish off.

ROSE MOTIF SET

EASY

Size	Finished Chest Measurement
2	19½" (49.5 cm)
4	21½" (54.5 cm)
6	23½" (59.5 cm)

Hat - 21½" (54.5 cm) circumference

Size Note: Instructions are written for size 2 with sizes 4 and 6 in braces { }. Instructions will be easier to read if you circle all the numbers pertaining to your child's size. If only one number is given, it applies to all sizes.

MATERIALS

- Medium Weight Yarn (MEDIUM 4)
  - [3½ ounces, 178 yards (100 grams, 163 meters) per skein]:
    - Pink **and** White - 2 skeins **each**
    - Green - 1 skein
- Crochet hook, sizes H (5 mm) **and** I (5.5 mm) **or** sizes needed for gauge
- Split-ring markers - 4
- ½" (12 mm) Buttons - 2
- Yarn needle
- Tapestry needle

Instructions begin on page 26.

GAUGE: With smaller size hook,
8 hdc and 5 rows = 2" (5 cm)

Gauge Swatch: 4" (10 cm) square
With smaller size hook and Green, work same as Square through Rnd 4.

STITCH GUIDE

V-STITCH *(abbreviated V-St)*
(Dc, ch 1, dc) in st or sp indicated.

Bodice is worked across the length to the finished chest measurement.

TOP

SQUARE

With smaller size hook and Green, ch 4, join with slip st to form a ring.

Rnd 1 (Right side)**:** Ch 3 **(counts as first dc, now and throughout)**, 2 dc in ring, (ch 2, 3 dc in ring) 3 times, ch 1, sc in first dc to form last ch-2 sp: 12 dc and 4 ch-2 sps.

Note: Loop a short piece of yarn around any stitch to mark Rnd 1 as **right** side.

Rnd 2: Ch 3, 2 dc in last ch-2 sp made, ch 1, ★ (3 dc, ch 2, 3 dc) in next ch-2 sp, ch 1; repeat from ★ 2 times **more**, 3 dc in same sp as first dc, ch 1, sc in first dc to form last ch-2 sp: 24 dc and 8 sps.

Rnd 3: Ch 3, 2 dc in last ch-2 sp made, ch 1, 3 dc in next ch-1 sp, ch 1, ★ (3 dc, ch 2, 3 dc) in next ch-2 sp, ch 1, 3 dc in next ch-1 sp, ch 1; repeat from ★ 2 times **more**, 3 dc in same sp as first dc, hdc in first dc to form last ch-2 sp: 36 dc and 12 sps.

Rnd 4: Ch 3, (2 dc, ch 2, 3 dc) in last ch-2 sp made, ch 1, (3 dc in next ch-1 sp, ch 1) twice, ★ (3 dc, ch 2, 3 dc) in next ch-2 sp, ch 1, (3 dc in next ch-1 sp, ch 1) twice; repeat from ★ 2 times **more**; join with slip st to first dc, finish off: 48 dc and 16 sps.

Rnd 5: With **right** side facing and smaller size hook, join White with slip st in any corner ch-2 sp; ch 3, 2 dc in same sp, ch 1, (3 dc in next ch-1 sp, ch 1) 3 times, ★ (3 dc, ch 2, 3 dc) in next ch-2 sp, ch 1, (3 dc in next ch-1 sp, ch 1) 3 times; repeat from ★ 2 times **more**, 3 dc in same sp as first dc, ch 1, sc in first dc to form last ch-2 sp; do **not** finish off: 60 dc and 20 sps.

STRIP

Row 1: Ch 1, sc in last ch-2 sp made, sc in each dc and ch-1 sp across to next ch-2 sp, sc in next ch-2 sp; leave remaining sts and sps unworked: 21 sc.

Row 2: Ch 2 **(counts as first hdc)**, turn; hdc in next sc and in each sc across.

Repeat Row 2 until Strip measures approximately 14{16-18}"/35.5{40.5-45.5} cm, ending by working a **wrong** side row.

Last Row: Ch 1, turn; sc in each hdc across; finish off leaving a long end.

Thread yarn needle with long end. With **wrong** sides together, beginning in second ch of corner ch-2 on Rnd 5 and matching sts and chs, whipstitch Last Row to dc and chs on Rnd 5 *(Fig. 4, page 32)*; finish off.

SKIRT

Rnd 1: With **right** side facing, using smaller size hook, working in end of rows across Strip and in sts and sps across Square, join Pink with sc at center back of Strip *(see Joining With Sc, page 32)*; ch 1, work 36{40-44} sc evenly spaced across to Square, work 21 sc evenly spaced across Square, work 38{42-46} sc evenly spaced across; join with slip st to first sc: 96{104-112} sc.

Rnd 2: Ch 3, dc in same st and in next sc, (2 dc in next sc, dc in next sc) around; join with slip st to first dc: 144{156-168} dc.

Rnd 3: Ch 4 **(counts as first dc plus ch 1, now and throughout)**, dc in same st, skip next dc, (work V-St in next dc, skip next dc) around; join with slip st to first dc: 72{78-84} V-Sts.

Rnds 4-16: Slip st in next ch-1 sp, ch 4, dc in same sp, work V-St in next ch-1 sp and in each ch-1 sp around; join with slip st to first dc.

Rnd 17: Ch 1, sc in same st and in each ch-1 sp and each dc around; join with slip st to first sc, finish off: 216{234-252} sc.

Rnd 18: With **right** side facing, join White with sc in same st as joining *(see Joining With Sc, page 32)*; sc in next sc and in each sc around; join with slip st to first sc.

Rnd 19: Ch 1, sc in same st and in each sc around; join with slip st to first sc, finish off.

Rnd 20: With **right** side facing, join Green with sc in same st as joining; sc in next sc and in each sc around; join with slip st to first sc, finish off.

Trim: With **right** side facing and using smaller size hook, working in end of rows on top of Bodice and across Square, join Green with sc at center back; work 75{83-95} sc evenly spaced around; join with slip st to first st, finish off: 76{84-96} sc.

SHOULDER TIE

With Trim at top and joinings at back, flatten Bodice. Place markers 1¾{2¼-2¾}"/4.5{5.5-7} cm from folded edge on **each** side of front and back.

With **right** side facing and using smaller size hook, join Pink with slip st in any marked sc; ch 42{42-46}, sc in second ch from hook and in each ch across, slip st in same st as joining slip st; finish off.

Repeat for remaining 3 Shoulder Ties.

FLOWER

With larger size hook and Pink, ch 4; join with slip st to form a ring.

Rnd 1 (Right side)**:** Ch 3, 17 dc in ring; join with slip st to first dc: 18 dc.

Note: Mark Rnd 1 as **right** side.

Rnd 2: Ch 5, skip next 2 dc, ★ slip st in next dc, ch 5, skip next 2 dc; repeat from ★ around; join with slip st to joining slip st: 6 ch-5 sps.

Rnd 3: ★ (Slip st, ch 3, 6 dc) in next ch-5 sp, slip st in next dc on Rnd 1 working around slip st on Rnd 2; repeat from ★ around; join with slip st to first slip st, finish off.

Using photo as a guide:
With Pink, sew button to center of Flower; sew Flower to center of Square.

HAT

Shown on page 6.

With larger size hook and White, ch 5; join with slip st to form a ring.

Rnd 1 (Right side)**:** Ch 3 **(counts as first dc)**, 17 dc in ring; join with slip st to first dc: 18 dc.

Note: Loop a short piece of yarn around any stitch to mark Rnd 1 as **right** side.

Rnd 2: Ch 4 **(counts as first dc plus ch 1, now and throughout)**, (dc in next dc, ch 1) around; join with slip st to first dc: 18 dc and 18 ch-1 sps.

Rnds 3-12: Slip st in first ch-1 sp, ch 4, (3 dc in next ch-1 sp, ch 1) around, 2 dc in same sp as first dc; join with slip st to first dc: 54 dc and 18 ch-1 sps.

Rnd 13: Ch 1, sc in same st, 2 sc in next ch-1 sp, (sc in next 3 dc, 2 sc in next ch-1 sp) around to last 2 dc, sc in last 2 dc; join with slip st to first sc: 90 sc.

Rnds 14-17: Ch 1, sc in same st and in each sc around; join with slip st to first sc.

Finish off.

Rnd 18: With **right** side facing, join Green with sc in same st as joining; sc in next sc and in each sc around; join with slip st to first sc, finish off.

FLOWER

Work same as Top.

Using photo as a guide:
With Pink, sew button to center of Flower; sew Flower to Hat.

RUFFLED SET

EASY

Size	Finished Length (from cuff to cuff)
2	19 3/4" (50 cm)
4	21 1/4" (54 cm)
6	22 3/4" (58 cm)

Hat - 21" (53.5 cm) circumference

Size Note: Instructions are written for size 2 with sizes 4 and 6 in braces { }. Instructions will be easier to read if you circle all the numbers pertaining to your child's size. If only one number is given, it applies to all sizes.

MATERIALS

Medium Weight Yarn (MEDIUM 4)
[6 ounces, 315 yards (170 grams, 288 meters) per skein]:
Red - 1{2-2} skein(s)
Bulky Weight Yarn (BULKY 5)
[2 1/2 ounces, 100 yards (70 grams, 91 meters) per skein]:
Variegated - 1 skein
Crochet hook, sizes H (5 mm) **and** I (5.5 mm) **or** sizes needed for gauge
Black pony bead
Yarn needle

GAUGE: With Red and larger size hook,
5 V-sts = 3 3/4" (9.5 cm);
7 rows = 3 1/2" (9 cm)

Gauge Swatch: 4 1/4" x 3 3/4" (10.75 cm x 9.5 cm)
Ch 20.
Rows 1-8: Work same as Shrug Body.
Finish off.

STITCH GUIDE

V-Stitch *(abbreviated V-St)*
(Dc, ch 1, dc) in st or sp indicated.

Treble Crochet *(abbreviated tr)*
YO twice, insert hook in st indicated, YO and pull up a loop, (4 loops on hook), (YO and draw through 2 loops on hook) 3 times.

Instructions begin on page 30.

SHRUG

BODY

With larger size hook and Red, ch 74{80-86}.

Row 1 (Right side)**:** Sc in second ch from hook and in each ch across: 73{79-85} sc.

Note: Loop a short piece of yarn around any stitch to mark Row 1 as **right** side.

Row 2: Ch 3 **(counts as first dc, now and throughout)**, turn; (skip next 2 sc, work V-St in next sc) across to last 3 sc, skip next 2 sc, dc in last sc: 23{25-27} V-Sts.

Rows 3 thru 16{17-18}: Ch 3, turn; work V-St in each ch-1 sp across to last dc, dc in last dc.

Row 17{18-19}: Ch 1, turn; 2 sc in first dc, sc in each dc and ch-1 sp across to last dc, 2 sc in last dc; finish off: 73{79-85} sc.

With **wrong** side together, fold Shrug in half lengthwise. Matching sts on last row with free loops of beginning ch *(Fig. 3, page 32)*, whipstitch across first 13{15-17} sts on each end to form sleeves *(Fig. 4, page 32)*, leaving center 47{49-51} sts unworked to form Body.

BODY TRIM

Rnd 1: With **right** side facing and larger size hook, join Variegated with sc in any st on Body opening *(see Joining With Sc, page 32)*; work 91{99-107} sc evenly spaced around; join with slip st to first sc: 92{100-108} sc.

Rnd 2: Ch 1, sc in same st, skip next sc, 5 dc in next sc, skip next sc, ★ sc in next sc, skip next sc, 5 dc in next sc, skip next sc; repeat from ★ around; join with slip st to first sc, finish off.

SLEEVE TRIM

Rnd 1: With **right** side facing, larger size hook, and working in end of rows, join Variegated with sc in any row; ch 1, work 43{51-59} sc evenly spaced around; join with slip st to first sc: 44{52-60} sc.

Rnd 2: Ch 1, sc in same st, skip next sc, 5 dc in next sc, skip next sc, ★ sc in next sc, skip next sc, 5 dc in next sc, skip next sc; repeat from ★ around; join with slip st to first sc, finish off.

Repeat for second Sleeve.

HAT

Shown on page 6.

BODY

With smaller size hook and Red, ch 5; join with slip st to form a ring.

Rnd 1 (Right side)**:** Ch 3 **(counts as first dc)**, 17 dc in ring; join with slip st to first dc: 18 dc.

Note: Loop a short piece of yarn around any stitch to mark Rnd 1 as **right** side.

Rnd 2: Ch 4 **(counts as first dc plus ch 1, now and throughout)**, (dc in next dc, ch 1) around; join with slip st to first dc: 18 dc and 18 ch-1 sps.

Rnds 3-12: Slip st in first ch-1 sp, ch 4, (3 dc in next ch-1 sp, ch 1) around, 2 dc in same sp as first dc; join with slip st to first dc: 54 dc and 18 ch-1 sps.

Finish off.

TRIM

With **right** side facing and larger size hook, join Variegated with sc in second dc of any 3-dc group *(see Joining With Sc, page 32)*; 5 dc in next ch-1 sp, skip next dc, ★ sc in next dc, 5 dc in next ch-1 sp, skip next dc; repeat from ★ around; join with slip st to first sc, finish off.

FLOWER

With Variegated and larger size hook, ch 5, join with slip st to form a ring.

Rnd 1 (Right side)**:** (Ch 3, 3 tr, ch 3, slip st) 6 times in ring; finish off.

Note: Mark Rnd 1 as **right** side.

With smaller size hook and Red, repeat for second Flower.

Place **wrong** side of Red Flower on top of **right** side of Variegated Flower, having Variegated Flower edges showing. Matching sts and Red, sew Flowers together.

Using photo as a guide: With Red, sew pony bead to center of Flower; sew Flower to Hat.

GENERAL INSTRUCTIONS

ABBREVIATIONS

ch(s)	chain(s)
cm	centimeters
dc	double crochet(s)
FPdc	Front Post double crochet(s)
hdc	half double crochet(s)
mm	millimeters
Rnd(s)	Round(s)
sc	single crochet(s)
sp(s)	space(s)
st(s)	stitch(es)
tr	treble crochet(s)
YO	yarn over

★ — work instructions following ★ as **many more** times as indicated in addition to the first time.

( ) or [ ] — work enclosed instructions **as many** times as specified by the number immediately following **or** work all enclosed instructions in the stitch or space indicated **or** contains explanatory remarks.

colon (:) — the number(s) given after a colon at the end of a row or round denote(s) the number of stitches or spaces you should have on that row or round.

CROCHET TERMINOLOGY		
UNITED STATES		INTERNATIONAL
slip stitch (slip st)	=	single crochet (sc)
single crochet (sc)	=	double crochet (dc)
half double crochet (hdc)	=	half treble crochet (htr)
double crochet (dc)	=	treble crochet(tr)
treble crochet (tr)	=	double treble crochet (dtr)
double treble crochet (dtr)	=	triple treble crochet (ttr)
triple treble crochet (tr tr)	=	quadruple treble crochet (qtr)
skip	=	miss

Yarn Weight Symbol & Names	LACE 0	SUPER FINE 1	FINE 2	LIGHT 3	MEDIUM 4	BULKY 5	SUPER BULKY 6
Type of Yarns in Category	Fingering, 10-count crochet thread	Sock, Fingering Baby	Sport, Baby	DK, Light Worsted	Worsted, Afghan, Aran	Chunky, Craft, Rug	Bulky, Roving
Crochet Gauge* Ranges in Single Crochet to 4" (10 cm)	32-42 double crochets**	21-32 sts	16-20 sts	12-17 sts	11-14 sts	8-11 sts	5-9 sts
Advised Hook Size Range	Steel*** 6,7,8 Regular hook B-1	B-1 to E-4	E-4 to 7	7 to I-9	I-9 to K-10.5	K-10.5 to M-13	M-13 and larger

*GUIDELINES ONLY: The chart above reflects the most commonly used gauges and hook sizes for specific yarn categories.

** Lace weight yarns are usually crocheted on larger-size hooks to create lacy openwork patterns. Accordingly, a gauge range is difficult to determine. Always follow the gauge stated in your pattern.

*** Steel crochet hooks are sized differently from regular hooks–the higher the number the smaller the hook, which is the reverse of regular hook sizing.

CROCHET HOOKS													
U.S.	B-1	C-2	D-3	E-4	F-5	G-6	H-8	I-9	J-10	K-10½	N	P	Q
Metric - mm	2.25	2.75	3.25	3.5	3.75	4	5	5.5	6	6.5	9	10	15

BEGINNER	Projects for first-time crocheters using basic stitches. Minimal shaping.
EASY	Projects using yarn with basic stitches, repetitive stitch patterns, simple color changes, and simple shaping and finishing.
INTERMEDIATE	Projects using a variety of techniques, such as basic lace patterns or color patterns, mid-level shaping and finishing.
EXPERIENCED	Projects with intricate stitch patterns, techniques and dimension, such as non-repeating patterns, multi-color techniques, fine threads, small hooks, detailed shaping and refined finishing.

GAUGE

Exact gauge is **essential** for proper fit or size. Before beginning your project, make the sample swatch given in the individual instructions in the yarn and hook specified. After completing the swatch, measure it, counting your stitches and rows or rounds carefully. If your swatch is larger or smaller than specified, **make another, changing hook size to get the correct gauge**. Keep trying until you find the size hook that will give you the specified gauge.

JOINING WITH SC

When instructed to join with sc, begin with a slip knot on hook. Insert hook in stitch or space indicated, YO and pull up a loop, YO and draw through both loops on hook.

JOINING WITH DC

When instructed to join with dc, begin with a slip knot on hook. YO, holding loop on hook, insert hook in stitch or space indicated, YO and pull up a loop (3 loops on hook), (YO and draw through 2 loops on hook) twice.

BACK LOOP ONLY

Work only in loop(s) indicated by arrow *(Fig. 1)*.

Fig. 1

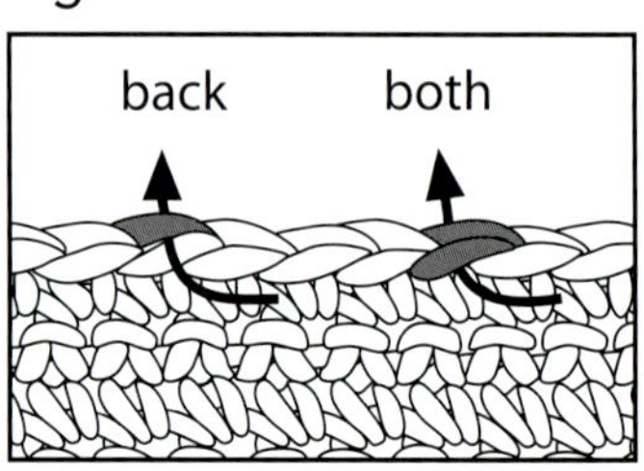

WORKING AROUND A SPACE

Work in space indicated, inserting hook in direction of arrow *(Fig. 2)*.

Fig. 2

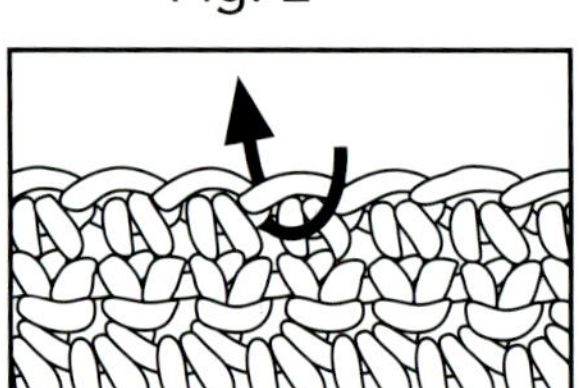

FREE LOOPS OF A CHAIN

When instructed to work in free loops of a chain, work in loop indicated by arrow *(Fig. 3)*.

Fig. 3

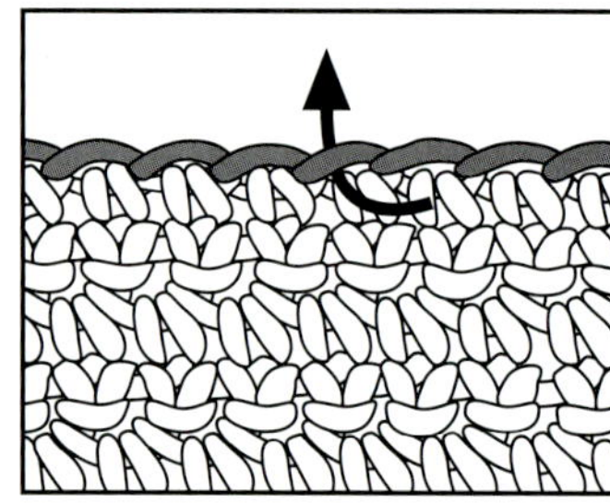

WHIPSTITCH

Place pieces with **wrong** sides together. Sew through both pieces once to secure the beginning of the seam, leaving an ample yarn end to weave in later. Insert the needle from **front** to **back** through **both** pieces *(Fig. 4)*. Bring the needle around and insert it from **front** to **back** through next loops of both pieces. Continue in this manner across.

Fig. 4

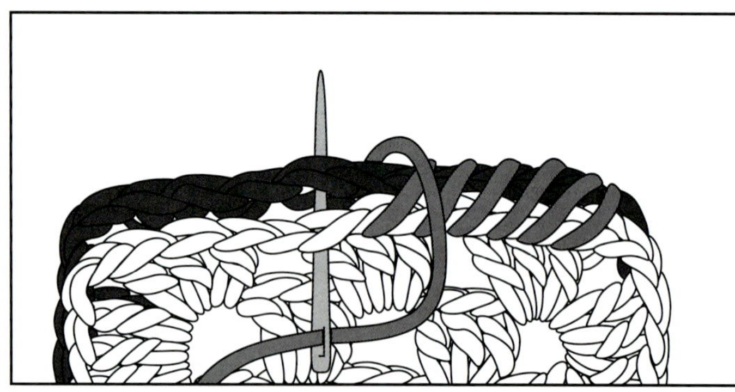